The Transformed Life

THE TRANSFORMED LIFE

A 30-Day Guide to Positive Change
and Fulfillment in Life

Kendra Watkins

CONTENTS

Introduction: IT'S TIME FOR CHANGE ix
Day 1: VALUE
        "Know Your Worth!" 1
Day 2: CHANGE
        "Repent and Turn Around!" 4
Day 3: THE POTTER'S TOUCH
        "I'm the Potter, You're the Clay" 7
Day 4: CHANGE
        "It's a Process!" 9
Day 5: GRACE
        "Endow Me" 12
Day 6: FAITH IS NECESSARY
        "O Ye of Little Faith!" 14
Day 7: FAITH
        "Romans 4:17" 17
Day 8: CHANGE YOUR MINDSET
        "A Set Mind" 20
Day 9: CHANGE YOUR MINDSET
        "Be Transformed!" 23
Day 10: CHANGE YOUR ENVIRONMENT
        "Come Out from Among Them!" 26

Day 11: COME OUT OF YOUR COMFORT ZONE
"You've Been There Too Long. What Is Keeping You There?"..28

Day 12: STAND OUT
"You Don't Fit in…Don't Compromise!" 31

Day 13: BE TRANSPARENT
"True Worship: I'm Naked!" 33

Day 14: MAKE CHANGES OR MAKE EXCUSES
"Wilt Thou Be Made Whole?"...................................36

Day 15: RELATIONSHIP OR ASSOCIATION?
"Get Alone with God!"...39

Day 16: CHANGE ATTRACTS OPPOSITION
"You Shall Receive Power!".......................................42

Day 17: BROKEN FOCUS
"Don't Look Back!"...45

Day 18: OVERCOMING MOMENTARY FAILURE
"Let It Refine You, Not Define You" 47

Day 19: GUARD YOUR GATES
"No Trespassing!"..49

Day 20: DEAL WITH YOUR ROOTS
"Stop Medicating Your Symptoms!"...........................51

Day 21: MATTERS OF THE HEART
"Issues of Life" 54

Day 22: DIE TO SELF
"It's Not About You!" 56

Day 23: GET SUPPORT
"I Need You!"..59

Day 24: FEAR DOWN, FAITH UP!
"No Fear! He Will Lead You" 61

Day 25: ENDURE THE PROCESS
"Persevere!" 64

Day 26: WHO ELSE IS IN THE FIRE?
"Untouched!" 67

Day 27: MAKE A DEPOSIT
"Inwardly Perishing" 69

Day 28: TEMPORARY CHANGE
"A Will Surrendered" 71

Day 29: NO FORMS
"Be the Change!" 74

Day 30: WHAT DO YOU SEE?
"God's Perspective vs. Your Perspective" 76

Day 31: SURPRISE! A BONUS DAY JUST FOR YOU!
BELIEVE IN YOURSELF!
"Faith It from Here" 79

Acknowledgments 83

Author's Bio 85

Contact the Author 87

The Transformed Life: A 30-Day Guide to Positive Change and Fulfillment in Life
by Kendra Watkins

Cover design, editing, book layout, and publishing services by KishKnows, Inc., Richton Park, Illinois.
708-252-DOIT
admin@kishknows.com, www.kishknows.com

ISBN 978-0-692-19516-1
LCCN 2018911173

All rights reserved. No part of this book may be reproduced, distributed, or transmitted in any form or by any means, including photocopying, recording, digital scanning, or other electronic or mechanical methods, without the prior written permission of the publisher, except in the case of brief quotations embodied in critical reviews and certain other noncommercial uses permitted by copyright law. For permission requests, please contact Kendra Watkins.

Some Scripture references may be paraphrased versions or illustrative references of the author. Unless otherwise specified, all other references are from **King James Version of the Bible**.

Copyright © Kendra Watkins 2018

Printed in the United States of America

INTRODUCTION

IT'S TIME FOR CHANGE

> "And be not conformed to this world: but
> be ye transformed by the renewing of your
> mind, that ye may prove what is that good,
> and acceptable, and perfect, will of God."
> **-Romans 12:2-**

You decided to pick up this book today. There was a reason for your actions. Do you need change? Do you want to be changed? Whatever your purpose was in picking up this book, you have made an excellent choice. I began this journey of transformation that impacted my life so profoundly in 2009. I got saved and baptized in Jesus' name, and I was filled with the precious gift of the Holy Spirit. From that day on, my life changed enormously. I was transformed miraculously. I am still in awe to this day of the wondrous work of God in my life alone. Before this happened, I had walked through the church doors one day without identity, without purpose or hope, without affirmation or agape love, and without so many other things. I was full of lies, hate, anger, low self-esteem, bitterness, pain, hurt, questions, and more.

I thank God for my pastors who embraced me with the love of God. I thank God for the leaders who, working together with God, reached inside me and helped me find my identity and purpose. They helped me find joy, hope, peace, and love in the Holy Spirit. They drew out the lies and filth that had kept my "true self" hidden for many years. I emphasize "true self" because a lot of times, what we become growing up is in result of what we saw, heard, and learned. We tend to be molded and shaped by it more than we know.

Okay, where was I? So, I thank God that they saw with the eyes of God Himself and embraced this damaged vessel with the Potter's loving hands. They didn't allow the state I was in to influence their thinking about how God could, with their help, bring about change in my life.

Now, it's my heart's desire for you to encounter what I encountered through this journey. It's my desire to see you embrace who you really are and to see you exchange your ashes for beauty. It's my heart's desire to see you free, healed, delivered, and being all that God has called you to be. You have a destiny to fulfill. This book is just one of the tools God will use to catapult you into it. This is only part of the process. After finishing the book, the rest of the process will require your dedication, commitment, discipline, and obedience.

I wrote this book in response to testimonies like these:

"Guard Your Gates" was such a powerful message that has forever changed my life, especially when Prophetess Kendra discussed the importance of guarding your ear gates. Coming from the inner city as an ex-drug dealer/player, I always listened to lust-driven, gangster, drug-promoting, and violent music. Even after being born again and filled with the precious gift of the Holy Ghost, I still compromised what I listened to while working out in the gym, believing that I needed the world's music to get me pumped or motivated for an explosive workout. The residue of the world was very evident in my walk with Christ, and I was ignorant of the impact it was having on my spiritual life. I give God the glory for releasing His supernatural Word to me through Prophetess Kendra one summer evening. She spoke so boldly and fervently when giving her testimony on how she put down the world's music because it was like poison to her spirit. The voice of the Lord spoke so clearly through her and told me it's time to stop serving two masters. Conviction fell so strongly on me that immediately at the end of the message I went through my phone and deleted every secular song off my playlist. This may not seem significant to your average Christian, but I tell you in my intimate time the Lord's voice suddenly became illuminated and magnified like a clashing symbol; and when He says in John 10:4 that His sheep know His voice, revelation of this Word opened the eyes of my understanding. I give God the glory for using Prophetess Kendra to release this life-changing message because it brought me closer to the Father." ~**Minister Vincent Casey, 37 years old (Edited)**

"One night while on YouTube, I ran across your YouTube page and the title simply stated, *Thirty Days of Change*. I was interested to see what you would say, so I clicked on the video and the rest is history. The words that were given to you by the Holy Spirit convicted me and tugged at my spirit so that I fell prostrate before the Father. The presence that fell upon me that night changed and shifted my life into a new dimension. I can't explain the encounter I had by those God-breathed words spoken through you. If this happened after listening to *one* of the *Thirty Days of Change*, I can only imagine the impact of all thirty days! I would encourage anyone to watch your videos and allow the Holy Spirit to change them." ~**Deondria West, 20 years old (Edited)**

"I am always blessed by Prophetess Kendra's broadcast. Truly, she is on fire for the Lord! I appreciate all the wisdom and strategies you have shared with us in the past year. You're definitely a blessing to the Body of Christ! I want to thank you for speaking into my life." ~**Tina Lowe, 43 years old (Edited)**

"God is a limitless God!!! For as long as I could remember, I struggled with fear. The spirit of fear had crippled me from walking in my God-given destiny and purpose. I struggled with fearing the unknown and if I wasn't in control of what happened in my life or around me, I made a conscious effort of not dealing with it.

As my journey began in ministry, I quickly gained the revelation that God had changed my name to "psalmist" and had anointed me to usher His people into His presence. But I could not fulfill the assignment until I let go of this thing called fear! Satan literally wanted to taint and steal my sound because he knew the greater that was in me before I did.

Through God's supernatural power, He sent me a lifeline and raised the standard. Tuning in to Prophetess Kendra's *Thirty Days of Change* via Periscope, she began to talk about how we serve a limitless God, and we must take the limits off Him in order to conquer what hinders us from moving forward in our God-given destiny!

The "I AM" used this woman of God's message to first break and fertilize my heart and as she declared Hebrews 11:6, that without FAITH, it is impossible to please God, the Word went out as an arrow of deliverance and pierced my soul. Having a heart to please God, I meditated on that Scripture day and night until it took root. I gained more revelation that not only is "fear" a spirit but it's about a simple "thought" that does not line up with the will of God. Proverbs 23:7 declares, "For as a man thinks in his heart so is he." I understand now that my limitless God has given us the authority and the keys/access to bind and loose!"

No longer am I a slave to fear because through the *Thirty Days of Change*, I was able to take the LIMITS OFF. Glory be to God. Hallelujah!" **~Psalmist Shay Adam, 30 Years Old (Edited)**

"The *Thirty Days of Change* was Heaven-sent. It impacted my life in a major way! One of the main things that changed my life was concerning the authority that God has given us to change our situation. At age sixteen, I lacked understanding of who I was in Christ. I didn't know my inheritance that I had received as a son of God. Due to this lack of knowledge, I was perishing in my spiritual walk. The enemy would toss me to and fro when the trials of life presented themselves in my circumstances. Oftentimes, I was left hopeless and helpless, and didn't know what to do and where to turn.

I knew that a supernatural, all-knowing God would not allow me to live my life like this. Listening to Prophetess Kendra on her *Thirty Days of Change* broadcast, I received the word that my soul longed for. She spoke passionately with a holy anger about us walking in the authority God has given us to change our situations. I realized that in the midst of situations that we go through, we either endure them until the end or suffer through them. Prophetess Kendra told us that because we are joint heirs with Christ, we don't have to suffer in situations; but just as the Bible says, "We can speak to the mountains" and watch God move on our behalf.

As quickly as she released this word, it was as if my spirit immediately grabbed a hold to it. Revelation was illuminated in my inner man. I realized that I didn't have to put up with just anything because the supernatural power of God has given me the authority to frame my world with my words and be who God has called me to be before the foundation of the world. Now, when I open my mouth, I speak with the authority God has given me and demons tremble. Bless His holy name!" ~**Kyle Davis, 17 years old (Edited)**

"While I was being attacked in my body by the enemy, I became hopeless. Many excuses and fears caused me to become stagnant. The words of God through Prophetess K gave me hope and charged me. They gave me hope to fight again. I began to know the true me the way God sees me. In the *Thirty Days of Change*, Prophetess K spoke the words that I must step into change and move by faith and not by what I see. That I must put faith in action and move past what I feel and only believe what God says about me in His Word and promises. God's Word is settled in Heaven. She said that I must speak the Word only according to my situation or circumstances, and that I must keep my faith and trust in God because without faith, it impossible to please my Daddy and I want to please Him. I take the Word now and I speak it out loud because faith comes by hearing and hearing the Word of God. I eat the Word, chew it, then swallow it, and bring it back up through speaking it. That is what cows do to get the full substance of their meal.

Because of the *Thirty Days of Change* with Prophetess K, I am back out there evangelizing and winning souls for Christ Jesus. I am singing with more passion and prophesying and bringing deliverance to God's people. The *Thirty Days of Change* with Prophetess K took me into a Kairos moment and catapulted me into new levels with God, and the time was redeemed for me. If you can watch the *Thirty Days of Change* that Prophetess Kendra taught on, please do. It will change your life." ~**Evangelist Calandra Parker, 46 years old (Edited)**

I received many of these through email when I begin to minister on Periscope. I received testimonials from people of different ages, different races, and different cultures, which encouraged me to write the book. Periscope is a social media app where you can connect with and reach people across the world. When I began teaching *Thirty Days of Change*, I didn't expect to write a book on it; but by the unction of the Holy Ghost and the cry of the people, I began to write this book.

Now, this is not your typical devotional. I desire you to take it one day at a time. Devote your time and self to each chapter. Sometimes, you'll need a day or so to digest and allow the revelation from some days to settle in your spirit, so you may possibly take more than thirty days to work through it. However you decide to go through the thirty days, make sure you make the most of them. Making the most of it is getting the desired results that you are in expectation for from reading this book—which is CHANGE! As you read these life-changing pages, you may notice that some information and Scriptures have been repeated. Studies have shown that repeating information is good for our memory, so eat everything you get. Some days will be longer than the others, but it's all good food to eat. I use the words *change* and *transformed* separately because I believe that they are two different things. When change hit my life, I was transformed from the inside out.

The word **change** means, "to make or become different," or it is the "act or instance of making or becoming different." *Change*, most of the time, deals with the outward effects. It's the act or instance dealing with something seen.

The word **transformed** means, "to make a thorough or dramatic change in the form, appearance, or character of." *Transformation* deals more with the inward change, which then influences the outside.

Because this is not your average devotional, I am going to need your undivided attention for the next thirty days. I've heard it said, "After thirty days, it becomes a habit; after sixty days, it becomes discipline; and after ninety days, it becomes a lifestyle." I want you to focus for the next thirty days, so that some bad habits can be replaced. At the end of each day you will find five parts where you get to apply what you have learned that day. There is the right information part, one for meditation, one for revelation, another for examination, and lastly, a part for declaration.

For the **right information** part, you will have Scriptures to read at the end of each day. It is by the Word that we are cleaned and purified. The Word is like a hammer, a fire, and a sword. It's quick and powerful, and it's just what we need to get the full benefit of transformation. Not only do we need the written Word of God, but we need revelation. This is what God builds His church on. Every part is essential for this book to benefit you. I am in expectancy for your transformation.

The second part is **meditation**. You will meditate on the material you've read that day and on the Scriptures that you've read. According to Dictionary.com, the word *meditate* means, "to think deeply or focus one's mind for a period of time, in silence or with the aid of chanting, for religious or spiritual purposes or as a method of relaxation. To think deeply or carefully about (something)." After you have read the Scripture out loud, get quiet and think on the Scripture. Replay it in your thoughts. You can even personify it. This part will prepare you for the next step.

The third part is **revelation**. *Revelation* means, "to uncover." It also means, "to bring something that was hidden or unknown to light." While reading through the section for that day and through the Scriptures, ask God to give you revelation about how they apply specifically to your life. Ask

Him to shine the light of His Holy Spirit into your heart and show you if anything that you've read applies to you. Ask Him if there's anything in your life that He wants to speak to you about.

The fourth part will be **examination**. You've read through the material, meditated on it, and looked for revelation. Now it's time to examine yourself. According to Dictionary.com, *examine* means, "to make a detailed inspection or investigation." This part is very important. You have to thoroughly examine yourself so that transformation can take place. Examine your heart. *Kardia* is the Greek word for heart, and it refers to the seat of who you are. It's the seat of your soul which is your mind, will, and emotions. Take a look into yourself. It's important to journal this part. Here are a few questions to help you start your journal: How do you see yourself? Did reading the Scripture shine light on any specific areas of your life? Did these areas hinder you from changing? What could be blocking your change?

Answering these questions will require you to be COMPLETELY HONEST AND REAL with yourself and God. How can you make changes using what God showed you? How will you take the action necessary to make this change possible in your life? I'm sure by now, you get the point of this part.

The fifth and last part will be **declaration**. When you declare something, you are announcing it publicly. You are acknowledging the possession of what you are declaring, so see your declaration manifesting as you say it. Using the day's reading and Scriptures as a guide, write a declaration. Then, you need to confess and pray this declaration. To create the transformation you desire, you MUST open your mouth and create your world using your God-given authority. You will see the manifestation of your declaration in your life.

I will write out the first day for you, so you can see how this works. I know it seems like a lot, but this will have a great impact on your "Transformed Life." This will produce true change from the inside out. Now let's get started!

DAY 1

VALUE

"Know Your Worth!"

First and foremost, I want you to know that you are worth it! I have heard it said, "If you don't believe in yourself, no one else will!" That is true for someone who doesn't know their worth. God believed in you on your worst and best days. He believed in you while you were a sinner. He believed in you when no one else believed in you, even yourself. Can I tell you your worth? Anthony Brown and Group Therapy's "Worth" says, "You thought I was worth saving, so You came and changed my life. You thought I was worth keeping, so You cleaned me up inside."

The part that really makes me smile is when the artist states, "You thought I was to DIE for, so You SACRIFICED YOUR LIFE!" That's how much you are worth. Your value is so great, that Jesus made Himself of no reputation, was made in the likeness of men, humbled Himself, and became obedient unto death and even the death of the cross. He went through pain and suffering just for you. He endured such heartache and affliction just for you. He bled and died just for you. Thank God, the story doesn't end there. The song continues: "So I could be free. So I could be whole." Jesus went and snatched the keys of hell, death, and the grave just for you, so that you don't have to be bound any longer. He then went and sat at the right hand of God where He makes intercession just for you. Wait…it doesn't stop there! He left a gift just for you—His Spirit—so that you would have the power to step into this transformed life He has prepared just for you. It's important that you know your worth and value, and that you are willing to take a step into change to become the person God has purposed and ordained you to be.

God created you on purpose. Therefore, you have a designed destiny to fulfill. The only way you will fulfill that purpose and destiny is by allowing change to invade your life and to be transformed into the sculptured, unique, peculiar person you were designed to be from the beginning. You were fearfully and wonderfully made with a purpose in the mind and heart of God. You are so valuable to God. He loves you with great love. If you're reading this devotional, you have stepped into a path that is going to change your life forever. You are so worth your change.

Enough is enough! No more existing and settling for less. It's time to live! It's time to let change in! It's time to say goodbye to the OLD YOU and hello to the NEW TRANSFORMED YOU! You are so much better than what people have limited you to be. You've been living your life by the wrong author, you've been trying to fulfill the dreams of others, and you've been trying to live up to the standards of others. You've been suffering too long in the life that others have built for you. You have hurt long enough. It's time to let go and let God take over. He's the Potter and you're the clay. Today, make the decision to walk into change. He's waiting for the boldness to arise in the individual who will dare to change. So, let's begin this journey…

Right Information: Psalms 139 and Philippians 2:5-11

Meditation: Think or ponder on the Scriptures.

Revelation: Let God speak to you through the Word.

Examination: How do you see yourself in today's reading? What areas were tender while you were reading? Make a thorough inspection of your heart.

Declaration: As I said, I will give you an example on Day 1 for declaration. You want to include the Scriptures in your declaration in any way you can. The Word is powerful all by itself. It's active when it's spoken out of the mouth of one who has faith and authority.

"God's love for me is still the same. Nothing can separate me from the love of the Father. I am loved by my Abba Father. I am valuable and worth dying for. According to Psalm 139, You know me. You have searched me and have known me. You know my down-sitting and uprising. You are acquainted with all of my ways. You fearfully and wonderfully created me with a purpose in mind. Your thoughts are good towards me and they are great. I will be changed. I will be transformed because I am worth it! God, I thank You that You are bringing change to me within and without. I make this declaration in total faith, knowing that You will do exceedingly and abundantly above all I ask or think. I declare that my life has changed. I am transformed from the inside out. The Potter's hand is on my life."

DAY 2

CHANGE

"Repent and Turn Around!"

Let's get down to business! What is change? True change is to be transformed from the inside out. This is the change that will last. This specific change will sustain you for the purpose and destiny God has intended for you. It's important to have effective change that will bring out your true identity in Christ.

I love to use the metaphor of a butterfly (this will be explained in depth on Day 4). The change begins on the inside and manifests on the outside.

Change is defined as "to make or become different; make or become a different substance entirely; transform, alter in terms of." Some synonyms for change are: alter, adjust, adapt, amend, modify, revise, refine, reshape, refashion, redesign, rework, reorder, revamp, remodel, transform, transfigure, metamorphose. As you can see, most of the synonyms have the prefix "re" at the beginning. This shows how, when change happens, you go from one state to another.

The focus of this book is to help restore you back into the original state that God had in mind for you before the foundation of this world. To help get you into your freedom, identity, purpose, and destiny. The Greek word for change is *Metaneo*, which means, "to change one's mind and purpose and to change the inner man (particularly, with reference to acceptance of the will of God)." It means to repent. *Meta* meaning "to change" and *Noieo* meaning "think." To think differently afterwards. After what? After you encounter truth.

It's important that as we go through the next thirty days, repentance takes place as God reveals things to you about yourself. True repentance puts you in a place of having a broken and contrite heart which God will not despise. He then draws near to you. You may be asking, "Why repentance?" Whenever you are exposed to truth, you need to acknowledge where you have been wrong and ask God to forgive you and to help you change your ways. God loves a heart that repents. Why? Because that is a heart that is prepared for Him. If you do not have a repentant heart, then your heart will become hardened and will reject truth when it tries to come in.

As the Scripture says, we fall short every day, both knowingly and unknowingly. You want to live a life of repentance. When you repent, you must do it from the heart. When it's done from the heart, you are more likely to sustain the change of mindset and behavior. If you don't root this change from the heart, you will go back to how things were before. Why? As my covering apostle states, "Anything that originates from the mind will NOT last!" What originates from the HEART will sustain us for permanent change. God is very clear about doing things from the heart. He says that we should love Him with ALL our heart. Why? Because when the heart is in it, it's real. It's not just lip service. He says in the Book of Isaiah that the people were coming to Him with lip service, but their hearts were far from Him.

God wants your heart because He then can truly have you. Your heart has to be a heart of repentance for it to really affect your life. As you repent and decide to change your mind and direction, you have to change your way of speaking and doing. We will get more into that later on. It's important for the next twenty-eight days that you put your heart into it!

Now that you understand what change is, I want you to position your mind and heart for the next twenty-eight days. I want you to make a commitment to be consistent with this book until the end of the course. Consistency will bring forth the results I am expecting for you. It was my consistency in the Word, prayer, and worship that brought forth my change and transformation. Write it as part of your declaration today that you will stay consistent and committed for the next twenty-eight days.

Right Information: Luke 10:27; Isaiah 29:13; Ephesians 4:21-24

Remember: Commit to reading the Scriptures I've given you for each day, meditating on them, and looking for revelation from God through them. Resolve to examine yourself in the light of what you have read, and declare them out loud, along with your intention to change in conformity with what you have learned.

Meditation:

Revelation:

Examination:

Declaration:

DAY 3

THE POTTER'S TOUCH

"I'm the Potter, You're the Clay"

We often try to make up this person we desire to be, or we try to pretend that we're someone we are not. Before you were formed in your mother's womb, God had already purposed you to be just what He desired. We are predestined to be conformed to the image of Christ. We only become the artwork that God desires when we quit trying to be the potter. Only God knows what the final artwork should look like. A lot of times, we try to mold ourselves into what we think we should be or what others have conjured us up to be. We try to please the imagination of what others desire. Can I tell you something? YOU WILL NEVER BE SATISFIED trying to fulfill the picture of what you or anyone else desires you to be. True joy and fulfillment come from being the original, unique, peculiar, and beautiful artwork God has purposed you to be.

Do not let the enemy lie to you any longer. You are destined to be great. Prove the enemy wrong and let God take the seat as your Potter. You will only fall into your true beauty by taking the position of the clay. Clay is soft and easily formed. Clay can be designed into anything the imagination can devise. God wants us to be like clay. We can't be hardhearted or resistant to the process. Lose your form and allow God to mold, shape, and make you into His masterpiece. Become like clay—soft and easily designed by the Potter's hand. That's why the Bible declares, "a broken and a contrite heart, O God, thou wilt not despise." (Psalm 51:17) Why? Because that's a heart that can easily be remolded, reshaped, and conformed into the image of His Son. Come to the Potter's house, let your guard down, surrender, and let the Potter take you in His hands. He's only sculpting what is already in you.

You have the ability to be just what God said you will be. He knows the end at the beginning. You are more than what the eyes can see!

Right Information: Isaiah 64:8; Jeremiah 18:1-4; Romans 8:2; Isaiah 46:10; Jeremiah 29:11

Meditation:

Revelation:

Examination:

Declaration:

DAY 4

CHANGE

"It's a Process!"

I have to let you know now—change is a process. Previously, I spoke about how change happens from the inside out. Change starts in the heart and it manifests outwardly. As I mentioned before, I like to use the metaphor of a transformed butterfly. There are different stages that a butterfly goes through before it transforms into a beautiful adult butterfly. Let's look at the different stages.

Stage 1. Egg: Birthing

Stage 2. Larva/caterpillar: Feeding

They do not stay in this stage for long. In this stage, all they do is eat. When the egg hatches, the baby caterpillar will start its work and eat the leaf it hatched onto. It's important for the mother butterfly to lay her eggs on the type of leaf the caterpillar will eat. Each type of caterpillar likes certain types of leaves. Since they are tiny and cannot travel to a new plant, the caterpillar needs to hatch on the correct kind of leaf it wants to eat. Caterpillars need to eat and eat so they can grow quickly. They instantly start growing and expanding when they start eating. They "molt" (shed their outgrown skin) several times as they grow.

Stage 3. Pupa: Transition

This is the stage where the caterpillar changes into a pupa, also known as a chrysalis. From the outside of the pupa, it looks as if the caterpillar may just be resting—but the inside is where all the action is happening. Inside the pupa, the caterpillar is rapidly changing. The caterpillar's old body parts are undergoing a remarkable transformation, called "metamorphosis" and are becoming the beautiful parts that make up the butterfly that will soon emerge. The tissues, limbs, and organs of a caterpillar have all been changed by the time the pupa is finished and is now ready for the final stage.

Stage 4. Adult: Reproduction

Finally, the caterpillar is done forming and changing inside the pupa. When the butterfly first emerges from the chrysalis, both wings are soft and folded against the body. This is because the butterfly had to fit all its new parts inside of the pupa. Once the butterfly has rested after coming out the chrysalis, it will pump blood into the wings to get them open and ready to fly. Adult butterflies are constantly looking to reproduce.

As you can see, every stage is necessary to get the final beauty of a butterfly. It's the same with us—the process is necessary for the final result. It will take sacrifice and patience. During the process, you can't become impatient because every stage is necessary. When you try to skip stages in the process, you will not have an effective transformation in your life. You will be missing something that was necessary for the final result, so it won't be complete.

Think of directions to make a cake. You need to follow every step in the recipe to get that good, delicious cake you desire in the end. It's the same with change and transformation. So, I want you to understand that change is a process. This is nothing that happens overnight. People who think they have changed overnight have been deceived. Just as a butterfly patiently goes through its different stages to become the beautiful butterfly it already is, so we go through this process as well. Why? Because God has already created us in His image, likeness, and nature. It has to be brought forth in the natural. We have to go through the process of change to bring forth the beauty that already exists. We have to break out of the barriers and limitations in each stage.

The Word declares, "...ye have NEED OF PATIENCE." (Hebrews 10:36) It also says, "But let patience have her perfect work, that ye may be perfect and entire, wanting nothing." (James 1:4) Why? Because after you have suffered a while, you will be perfect and established, wanting nothing. So, let change have its perfect work in you that you can transform into the peculiar, unique, chosen, fearfully and wonderfully made individual He has purposed in His heart.

Right Information: Hebrews 10:35-39; James 1:4

Meditation:

Revelation:

Examination:

Declaration:

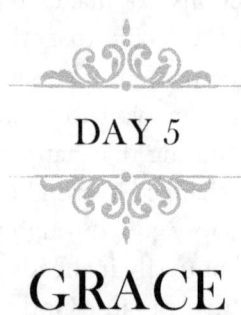

DAY 5

GRACE

"Endow Me"

Our flesh is weak, but the Spirit is always willing. (See Matthew 26:41) I want to begin with this because we need the power to be transformed and changed from the inside out. If you really want change to impact your life, I want you to ask God to endow you with power to be transformed. Many times, we try in our own strength and fail over and over, and then we give up and say there is no hope. I am confident that if you ask God to endow you with power, He will do it. He will empower you to walk in this transformed life that you desire. He declared in the book of Acts, "But ye shall receive power, after that the Holy Ghost is come upon you…" (Acts 1:8). The power to be a witness, to overcome, and to be transformed.

Not only do you have the POWER, but you have GRACE! Oh, how I thank God for grace. I loved how my apostle put it one Sunday morning, "Grace is the power, the ability to overcome or conquer what we can't in our flesh or own strength." Power with grace is necessary for you to be transformed from the inside out. Ephesians 2:8 declares,

"For by grace are ye saved through faith; and that not of yourselves: it is the gift of God." When you step into your salvation by receiving Jesus Christ as your Lord and Savior, believing in your heart and confessing with your mouth that Jesus died for your sins and was raised from the dead, you obtain grace.

After making that great confession, you are baptized in the beautiful name of Jesus Christ for the remission of your sins and are filled with the precious gift of the Holy Spirit. You can now access His power. Now, you are equipped to walk in this transformed life.

If you continue to try in your own strength, you will never walk into your transformed life. Be endowed with power or get a fresh encounter today that will charge you to walk out this transformed life. You need to be endowed with power!

Right Information: Acts 1:8; Romans 10:19-10; 2 Corinthians 3:16-18

Meditation:

Revelation:

Examination:

Declaration:

DAY 6

FAITH IS NECESSARY

"O Ye of Little Faith!"

When you desire to do things outside of the norm, you will need faith to accomplish this. A lot of times, we stay in cycles and bondage that keep transformation from happening because we don't believe it in our hearts. If you believe that you're no good, then you will be no good. You have to believe for the better. We only go so far based on our mindset. Faith takes us into the impossible. What seemed impossible before will become possible with faith. You have to believe in your heart that you are worth what God has designed you to be. We often have no faith when it comes to our personal life-changing for the good. We can encourage everyone else, but when the light is on us, we don't believe. If you have faith the size of a mustard seed, God can move with that. We all have been given a measure of faith that God desires for us to increase.

Romans 12:2 tells us that we are transformed by the renewing of our mind. This is the key not only to your transformation but to your faith because faith comes by hearing and hearing by the Word of God. If you change the way you think, you will change the way you talk, act, walk...you'll change your life! But it all goes back to faith... Do you believe? I'm going to give you some words formed by using the letters from the word FAITH that will help you build your faith. Without faith, it's impossible to please God (see Hebrews 11:6). It's also impossible to change and to be transformed. It takes faith, a belief system, to do something new. Doing new things can be scary, but if you have faith, you're not alone.

To help us understand what faith is, we can look at the first letters of the word. The first letter, **F**, stands for the **F**ear of the Lord. The fear of God is necessary for your faith to increase. To fear God is to reverence, respect, honor, and worship Him. We can't truly fear God until we love Him from the heart. We have to truly love God to truly fear Him. Our faith lacks because we don't fear God Who gives us the grace to increase our faith. When you love God with all your heart, mind, soul, and strength, you can embrace the fear of God. There is no lack for those who fear Him. If we learn to honor and fear God, we could walk in great transformation. Based on the awesomeness of God, I believe, He's worthy of our respect, reverence, honor, and worship. If you just think on the Scriptures that magnify His goodness, you can really get an honor and love for God. In Psalms 8:4, it states, "What is man that thou art mindful of him?" How He fearfully and wonderfully made us, how He has us in the palms of His hands...Just meditate on His goodness and the fear of God can be enriched in you. Get a hunger for the fear of God and act on that hunger. Begin to fear God, and He will manifest Himself to you. When God manifests Himself to you, transformation is bound to happen. I want you to really focus on the fear of the Lord. Get an awe for God. Spend some time with Him today. Love Him and ask Him to give you a fear for Him. We'll look at the second letter in "FAITH" tomorrow!

Right Information: Hebrews 11:6; Psalm 34:9; Psalm 86:6-7; Isaiah 29:13; Psalm 8:4; Psalm 139:14

Meditation:

Revelation:

Examination:

Declaration:

DAY 7

FAITH

"...calleth those things which be
not as though they were."
-Romans 4:17-

Let's continue with the "FAITH" letters! The **F** in faith stands for the **F**ear of the Lord. The second letter in the word *faith* is **A**, which stands for **A**cknowledgment. The Hebrew word *Yada,* commonly known as "acknowledge," means, "to regard" or "to recognize." Webster's dictionary states that *acknowledge* means, "To recognize as a fact or truth; to declare one's belief in; as to acknowledge the being of God.

When you acknowledge God for who He is, He becomes just that for you. Proverbs 3:6 says that if we acknowledge Him in all our ways, then He will direct our paths. Proverbs 16:3 also states that if we commit our plans or works to the Lord, then He will bring them to pass. This is the power of acknowledging God. When you acknowledge God, you're simply relinquishing your own will for His will. If I acknowledge my situations or circumstances to Him, I'm saying, "God, Your Word declares that You are Jehovah Jireh, my provider, so I acknowledge my circumstances and situations to You so that You may move in my favor. I choose to step away so that Your will may be done." Because if I acknowledge Him and put my situation and circumstances at His feet in faith of who He is, then He is able to work because I choose to acknowledge Him and move out of the way. Now He can act on my behalf. I trust the process and wait on Him to intervene. He manifests Himself, and now my faith has increased because of it. When we acknowledge God, we build our faith. When we learn to acknowledge Him more, we will be able to see heaven on earth.

The next letter is **I** for **I**ntimacy. To be intimate with God is to know Him personally. When we are intimate with God through prayer and worship, He reveals Himself to us. We get to know Him for who He really is. Through intimacy, we are perfected in His image and likeness. Through intimacy, we become one with Him as His heart desires us to be. Intimacy is where we meet God face to face. When we meet Him face to face, He reveals Himself to us. He speaks to us and when He speaks, we can act with confidence on what He said. We know that "God is not a man, that He should lie; neither the son of man, that He should repent…" (Numbers 23:19) One thing we can rest assured of is that if He said it, it shall come to pass. He is faithful and He keeps His promises. Intimacy causes our faith to be built up because we are in the very atmosphere of faith through intimacy.

T is for **T**hanksgiving. The first act of your faith is you giving thanks to God after your petition or declaration to God for anything. When you praise or give thanks before you see anything in the natural, it is a response to God that by faith, you know He has already done it. Because Faith is NOW! The Scripture states that NOW, faith is the SUBSTANCE of things HOPED for in the EVIDENCE of things NOT seen. It's NOW!

This brings us to the last letter, **H**, which stands for **H**ope. *Hope* is defined as "a feeling of EXPECTATION and desire for a certain thing to happen." I love the second definition which says that hope is "a feeling of trust." Faith believes in who God says He is and trusts His Word. You believe by faith the petitions and see them by faith and expect to have it in the natural. You TRUST that if God said it, then it is so. God said that His promises are YES and AMEN! Just believe and ANYTHING IS POSSIBLE!

Right Information: Romans 4:17; Proverbs 3:6; Proverbs 16:3; Numbers 23:19

Meditation:

Revelation:

Examination

Declaration:

DAY 8

CHANGE YOUR MINDSET

"A Set Mind"

A mindset is simply a set mind. Previously, we talked about the importance of renewing your mind. You will not be able to walk in the new with your old mindset. For example, if your mind is set on the words that were spoken to you when you were young such as, "You are a failure, you'll never be anything, you're just like your daddy..." etc., then that will be your mindset. Since your mind is set on that, you will think like that. You will think thoughts of failure, inadequacy, and disqualification. These are the spoken living words which have shaped you into who you are. The words your mind is set on are the words that hold you in your past, your bondage, your hurt, and your captivity if you decide not to change your mind to the truth of God's Word. Your mind has the power to transform your life.

Your mind has the power to change you from the inside out. Your mind has the power to catapult you into a journey of transformation. Glory! The power of one word can shift you into a new realm of thinking. All you need is one word from the Spirit of Truth to disrupt the lies that have built your mindset! 2 Corinthians 10:4 tells us that using spiritual weapons, we have the power to pull down strongholds and bring our thoughts into captivity to the obedience of Christ. *Strongholds* in this passage simply means the fortresses or words that have been built in your mind to detour you from your purpose. The words that have shifted your mindset from truth to lies. The words that have stripped your true identity from you. The words that have robbed you of your joy, peace, and love. The words that have taken away your confidence. The words that turned you from light to darkness.

The good news is that we have the power to tear down and destroy the fortresses the enemy started building in our childhood. A lot of times, when you get free from the strongholds of lies, you will see many of them started when you were young. The enemy targets us when we are young. Therefore, it's important to cover your children and to build them up with positive words, but that's a subject for another time.

So, God has given us power to change our mindset. Jeremiah 1:10 states, "See, I have this day set thee over the nations and over the kingdoms, to root out, and to pull down, and to destroy, and to throw down, to build, and to plant." You can stop the fortress from growing from this day forward. The strongholds in your mind have been built from your culture, ethnicity, upbringing, education, and many other things. They've been built on hurt, pain, rejection, etc. Today, I want to expose you to the power that God has given to pull them down. We can eradicate every lie, death word, and spoken curse that was spoken over us. You don't have to think the same from this day forward. Break out of the prison and choose to be free. Choose to change the channel. As a matter of fact, choose to write a new story. Start today! Begin to write your true story by beginning to change your mind!

Right Information: 2 Corinthians 10:4; Jeremiah 1:10; Joshua 1:8

Meditation:

Revelation:

Examination:

Declaration:

DAY 9

CHANGE YOUR MINDSET

"Be Transformed!"

Transformation cannot be sustained if you don't change your mindset. Your mindset has everything to do with your walking into your transformed life. The mind is more powerful than we think. If you change your mindset, you can change your life. The Word declares, "For as he thinketh in his heart, so is he." (Proverbs 23:7) You are your very thoughts. Your thoughts are evident in your life. Do you want to know how you've been thinking? Look at your life. True transformation comes in its fullness when you decide to change your mind.

The best transformation begins in the presence of God and continues in the Word of God. When you have lived a certain way for so long, you have taken on the mindset, character, attributes, nature, and ways of that which you have conformed to. The Word commands, "And be not conformed to this world, but be ye transformed by the renewing of your mind…" (Romans 12:2) and also states, "For whom He did foreknow, He also did predestinate to be conformed to the image of His Son." (Romans 8:29)

How do we know what that image looks like? By looking in the Word of God. Everything pertaining to your new life in Christ Jesus is in the blueprint, which is the Word of God. You have to find out who you are, who God is, what He has promised, what's rightfully yours, the power that lies within, and so much more. When you know, then you can be conformed to those things.

"My people are destroyed for lack of knowledge." (Hosea 4:6) You are not because you know not! What you don't know can keep you in bondage and stuck in your old ways. If you don't know, how do you expect to be? It wasn't by coincidence that Jacob had Joseph eating and studying the Word. It wasn't by coincidence that God told Joshua to meditate on His word day and night. (See Joshua 1:8) It wasn't by coincidence that God told Ezekiel to eat the scroll. (See Ezekiel 3:3) We need to feed on the Word daily. Just like we need our natural food every day to sustain us, we need our daily bread which is the Word, to sustain our transformed life in Christ Jesus. "But He answered and said Man shall not live by bread alone, but by every word that proceedeth out of the mouth of God." (Matthew 4:4)

We have the *logos* and *rhema* words that we need to sustain our transformed life. *Logos*, being the written Word of God; and *rhema*, being the spoken or revealed Word of God. When you eat and study the Word of God, make sure you get an understanding of it and a revelation of what it means for your life. Why? Because that's the seed that's planted in your heart. In the parable that Jesus told, the seed that fell by the wayside was the seed that had no understanding or revelation. What am I saying? You need the Word! Don't become lazy when it comes to spending time in the Word. Ask God for a new hunger for the Word of God. I prophesy that you will have a hunger and thirst for the Word like never before. That the Word will be like fire in you, causing change to manifest in your life. Your renewed mind is necessary for this transformed life.

Dr. Carol S. Dweck is one of the world's leading researchers in the field of motivation and is a professor of psychology at Stanford University. She believes that we basically have either a **fixed mindset** which implies that we believe that our attributes and abilities are inherently fixed and unchanging, or alternatively, we have a **growth mindset** that means that we believe our talents and abilities can be improved and developed. A person with a fixed mindset won't go beyond their level of ability because they think that that's it. They won't face challenges. A person with a growth mindset will look for challenges and will push to go beyond their limitations. A lot of times, we don't change because we have a fixed mindset that what we started with is all we have. BUT NOT SO! OUR GOD IS ABLE TO DO EXCEEDINGLY AND ABUNDANTLY ABOVE ALL WE CAN ASK OR EVER THINK. I PROPHESY THAT YOU ARE BREAKING OUT OF THE LIMITATIONS OF A FIXED MINDSET! IN JESUS' NAME!

Right Information: Romans 8:29; Romans 12:2; Proverbs 23:7; Hosea 4:6; Joshua 1:8; Ezekiel 3:3; Matthew 4:4

Meditation:

Revelation:

Examination:

Declaration:

DAY 10

CHANGE YOUR ENVIRONMENT

"Come Out from Among Them!"

How can you expect change if you stay in the same environment? It's not possible! Your environment is a great component in the change and transformation manifesting in your life. If I had stayed around the same friends who introduced me to smoking, drinking, and clubbing, I would have never broken free from the chains that held me bound. If you stay around negative influences, you will soon become a victim of those negative influences. What you surround yourself with will impact your life and affect your thinking, speaking, behavior, and even your character. No matter how much effort you put into trying to change, it will be ineffective because the familiarity or commonness of that environment will influence you or keep you in bondage.

It wasn't a coincidence that some of the great men in the Bible were called out of their hometowns to serve God. When God called Abraham, he was told to leave all that he knew to become the father of many nations. He had to come out of his familiar environment because what was in that environment wouldn't have been conducive to this change that God was bringing him into. Elisha and the disciples were called away from the environment that they knew so well because God knew it wasn't beneficial for the change that was getting ready to take place.

That's why Jesus stated, "Pick up your cross, deny your flesh, and FOLLOW ME!" because you have to come outside of the norms. You have to be willing to change your circle, association, and your location. If you really desire true change to be your portion, do not think that staying in the same environment will benefit you. It will only hinder you. That's why God declares in His Word: "…what fellowship hath righteousness with unrighteousness? and what communion hath light with darkness?" (2 Corinthians 6:14)

I had to change everything around me to really embrace true change. No matter how you try to justify it, the same environment and people will hinder the process of change and keep you in bondage. You have to come out of that place.

BE FREE TO CHANGE AND TRANSFORM!

Right Information: Genesis 12:1-5; 1 Kings 19:20-21; 2 Corinthians 6:14-17

Meditation:

Revelation:

Examination:

Declaration:

DAY 11

COME OUT OF YOUR COMFORT ZONE

*"You've Been There Too Long.
What Is Keeping You There?"*

Many times, we forfeit change because we are comfortable where we are. We don't always know that change is the key to unlocking the next phase in our lives. We can get so caught up in the way we are used to doing things that when God calls for something new, we are slow to respond because it requires something different. That is why God hates religion. Religion blocks the heart and mind of God. Religion keeps God and the Holy Spirit out of the picture. Religion and tradition overthrow the will of God. The Word declares, "That except your righteousness shall exceed the righteousness of the scribes and Pharisees, ye shall in no case enter into the kingdom of heaven" (Matthew 5:20). The scribes and Pharisees were a sect of self-righteous religious people who couldn't see Jesus in front of them.

You can't expect anything different to happen if you're doing exactly as you've always done. When change happens, it's new to you. I heard a man say, "If you never jump, how can you soar?" If you don't embrace uncomfortable situations, you will stay conformed to the likeness of this flesh. You won't be transformed by staying in the emotion, mindset, and will that this flesh desires.

The man at the pool of Bethesda was asked, "Wilt thou be made whole?" (John 5:6) Why? Because he had been sitting at the pool for thirty-eight years. His response was simply an excuse that nobody else had helped him. He used what people had done to him as an excuse for not getting into the water. That sounds like us! We blame everyone else for who we are and where we are in life. The moral of the story is that you didn't come out of your comfort zone. The only thing that hindered this man from embracing the transformation that awaited him was his comfort zone. He was so use to being the victim, so use to not being able to walk, and not being able to take care of himself, that when the time came for him to embrace change, he used excuses to explain why he could not have what God had promised him.

So, I ask you, "What hinders you from change?" Are you use to depending on people? Are you use to not having to do things for yourself? Are you use to the attention being on you because of your condition? Are you use to not taking responsibility? Are you afraid? Does the unknown scare you? I want you to be real with yourself. Why are you still there after thirty-eight years? The man at the pool didn't take responsibility for his own limitations! He didn't take responsibility for why he was still there after thirty-eight years! We cannot blame everyone else when it comes to breaking free from our bondage, limitations, and comfort zones. Instead of us moving forward, we tend to hold on to what happened in our past. We use the same excuses about why we are not whole and even about why we are still where we were thirty-eight years ago. Maybe it hasn't been thirty-eight years for you. What about twenty? Fifteen? Ten? Five?

Even Two? Whatever the case may be…IT'S TIME FOR CHANGE! WILL YOU BE MADE WHOLE TODAY?

    I'm not just talking naturally, but spiritually as well. It's time for you to be the person that God called you to be. It's time for you to embrace YOU! "Rise, take up thy bed, and walk!" (John 5:8)

Right Information: Matthew 5:20; John 5:6-8

Meditation:

Revelation:

Examination:

Declaration:

DAY 12

STAND OUT

"You Don't Fit in...Don't Compromise!"

When change starts impacting your life, you start finding out who you really are. A lot of times, we can spend our lives being the character in someone else's book. When transformation starts manifesting, there is some stripping and exposing of the lies, and there is a break out of the truth. You're not the same person that walked in when you come out of the presence of God. Now that change is impacting your life, you're not fitting in anymore. I can identify with this! When true transformation hit my life, I started to lose the circle of friends I had once trusted in. My circle got smaller and smaller as transformation took over my life.

The Word declares that we are Chosen, Royal, and Peculiar! (See 1 Peter 2:9) If you look at those words, none of them look like words that would make you common in the bunch. The story of the three Hebrew boys is a great example. (Daniel 3) They had been transformed and changed by God. They had their minds renewed and had learned the truth that kept them free. In the midst of people who wanted to compromise to fit in with everyone else, they stood out in the midst of the crowd. They knew that bowing to an idol was not their Father's desire, so they obeyed the commandment of God. They chose not to compromise. When everyone else was bowing to the idol, they chose to stand out. Because they stood out among the other people, they were thrown into a fiery furnace that was designed to kill them. BUT GOD IS FAITHFUL!

People try to keep the crowds of people by compromising, but God is not pleased with that. Your obedience is better than your sacrifice. Trying to fulfill the desires of flesh will get you out of position.

The story of Saul is a great example. (1 Samuel 15) He compromised, and it cost him his crown. We always have a choice! It depends on our obedience or disobedience—whether we will make the right one or not. We have to understand that as we go down this journey of change, we will not fit into the crowd. Today, we have so many people forfeiting transformation because it causes them not to fit in and be different. It's okay to be different! Be the trendsetter! I want you to know that the flesh is never satisfied anyway, so why take the time to try to please it? I challenge you this week to be different.

Right Information: 1 Peter 2:9; Daniel 3; 1 Samuel 15

Meditation:

Revelation:

Examination:

Declaration:

DAY 13

BE TRANSPARENT

"True Worship: I'm Naked!"

If you truly want to be transformed from the inside out, you have to be real from the inside out. *Transparent* is defined as "allowing light to pass through so that objects behind can be distinctly seen." One of the biggest hindrances of transparency is PRIDE. Ego is a KILLER! We prefer to put on a show and pretend that we have it all together instead of being broken and contrite. Pride doesn't want anyone to see the real you. Know this: God knows everything about us. He's omniscient, which means that He's ALL-KNOWING. You can think no one sees or knows, but God sees and knows all. If you can't keep it real with yourself and God, you will never come into a place of transformation.

God seeks the truth from us, so that we can know what's in us. Deuteronomy 8:2 says, "And thou shalt remember all the way which the Lord thy God led thee these forty years in the wilderness, to humble thee, and to prove thee, to know what was in thine heart, whether thou wouldest keep his commandments, or no." Your transparency isn't for anyone else's benefit BUT YOURS! You have to be in the place where you're okay with being naked before God. You don't have to be afraid to be real about yourself. God is love. You don't have to feel shameful or guilty about what you are dealing with or have dealt with in your past. God takes the ugly and beautifies it. He declared, "I'll give you beauty for your ashes." (See Isaiah 61:3) We must be okay with giving Him our ashes, so He can transform our life and beautify it.

I used to have an issue with being transparent. One day, unctioned by the Holy Ghost, I began to testify and encourage an individual in a way in which I then became transparent. After I had finished ministering to this individual, I felt even more freedom. It was as if, through my transparency, I had come into a greater level of freedom. I used to be ashamed of my past, but I remembered that when the Lord called me, He also JUSTIFIED me which put me in a place of innocence as if I had done nothing wrong. I had to get true revelation of that because we must know there is no condemnation for those who walk by the Spirit. (See Romans 8:1) You don't have to keep walking in condemnation. Go ahead and set yourself free by being transparent with yourself and God.

When Adam and Eve went against the commandment of God, they hid themselves from the presence of the Lord. That's what we do when we have done wrong. God called for Adam, "Where are you?" He was beckoning him to be real with Him. He asked Adam, "Hast thou eaten of the tree, whereof I commanded thee that thou shouldest not eat?" (Genesis 3:11) The question wasn't for God—it was for Adam. His first response was to blame it on Eve. A lot of times, we try to blame and expose everyone else, so we can stay out of the light. Adam chose to blame his actions on someone else rather than to be transparent and say, "Yes, I did it. Forgive me." God just wanted the truth out of Adam. It wasn't that God didn't know. He wanted to prove to Adam what was in his heart.

He didn't want Adam hiding; He wanted the truth. God doesn't treat us as our sins deserve. He desires us to be free in Him. He wants a relationship with us. In order for you to get to a place of true transformation, you have to open up your heart and get naked before God. QUIT HIDING AND BE REAL WITH YOURSELF! If you stay hidden and continue to lie to yourself, you'll eventually start believing the lie. Make a decision to be transparent. No more hiding behind the mask, the pain, the hurt, and lies. Open up so that God can come in…and change you.

Right Information: Psalm 139; Deuteronomy 8:2; Isaiah 61:3; Genesis 3:1-15

Meditation:

Revelation:

Examination:

Declaration:

DAY 14

MAKE CHANGES OR MAKE EXCUSES

"Wilt Thou Be Made Whole?"

Excuses are suggestions that the enemy releases into your thoughts to keep you from being transformed. If you always have an excuse for your conformity, religion, bondage, attitude, etc., then change will never be able to impact your life. *Excuse* is defined as "to try to remove the blame." It's our duty to walk in transformation. "Be ye transformed, by the renewing of your mind." (Romans 12:2) There is something required of us to walk in transformation which is renewal of the mind. God desires for us to be whole and delivered. If we want to be transformed, we have to receive our wholeness. The Greek word for salvation is *soteria*, which means, "to be delivered; to be whole in spirit, soul, and body."

"And the very God of peace sanctify you wholly; and I pray God your whole spirit and soul and body be preserved blameless unto the coming of our Lord Jesus Christ." (1 Thessalonians 5:23) Salvation has not just been provided for us to go to heaven, but for us to walk in newness of life and to bring heaven to earth. If we are in bondage, then we aren't able to do kingdom business. Wholeness is necessary for transformation to take place. If we keep making excuses about why we can't do something or be something, we won't obtain fullness of life in Christ Jesus.

In John Chapter 5, we read about a man who had been at the pool of Bethesda for thirty-eight years. He watched everybody else prosper, advance, and get healed for thirty-eight years. Jesus asked him, "Wilt thou be made whole?" After thirty-eight years of sitting and not making any change, Jesus asked him, in essence, "Will you be made whole? Are you going to be transformed by the power of the Holy Ghost?" What the man began to do was make excuses about why nothing had happened for him yet. He blamed others for why he wasn't able to obtain his wholeness. If you continue with excuses, then change will not impact your life. You have to quit being dependent on others so much and take hold of God Almighty who is able to change your life in a moment. No more excusing yourself. Even in our weakness, God said that He's our strength. Elijah went into a cave based on excuses because he felt that he couldn't do what was necessary to conquer his enemy. After so long, God told him he had to get out of the cave.

Someone else we can look at is David. David had just experienced the pain of a lifetime in losing his son. He had so many reasons to be depressed and to stay at home and sleep, but he didn't. He rose up, put on a new garment, and moved forward. We have to be like David and rise up and get to business. Let's make changes!

Kendra Watkins

Right Information: Romans 12:2; 1 Thessalonians 5:23

Meditation:

Revelation:

Examination:

Declaration:

DAY 15

RELATIONSHIP OR ASSOCIATION?

"Get Alone with God!"

We often find ourselves gravitating towards people because they have something we desire. We have a circle of friends or associates that we love to be around because it's always good vibes being in their midst. We find ourselves having that one friend that we stick close to and spill our heart to because of the comfort and freedom we feel when we are with them.

When it comes to our relationship with God, however, we tend to procrastinate when it comes to spending time with Him. One thing we have to understand is that He created us, so He knows us better than we know ourselves. If we lack a relationship with God, we will lack transformation and change in our lives. It's so important that our relationship with Him be a priority in our lives. "But seek ye first the kingdom of God, and His righteousness; and all these things shall be added unto you." (Matthew 6:33) It's only that as we know the Father, that we know who we are. A lot of times, we treat God as just another individual who we can talk to when we feel like it. The Word declares, "I never knew you." (Matthew 7:23) Why? Because we never really got into a relationship with Him. We tend to get busy in ministry, wanting the fame, and wanting the acceptance, but we miss our first priority which is the relationship with our Abba Father. Relationship with Him is a key element in your transformation.

Associates come together because they share the same common purpose. We treat God like this at times. When we want or need something, we go and cry out to God. When everything is going well, we fall back into our old habit of not communicating with God. What if you went to God on a daily basis just to be with Him because of the relationship? You would see your life change dramatically. When He visits us in our secret place, He transforms us. David said, "The hills melted like wax at the presence of the Lord, at the presence of the Lord of the whole earth." In the same way, our problems and sins melt away when we rest in our Father's presence. Something happens when you are in the presence of God.

Apostle Guillermo Maldonado of King Jesus Ministries in Miami, Florida, gives seven key components which make up a true relationship. *Communication* is the main foundation of a relationship. So if you're not communicating with God daily through prayer, then how are you in relationship with Him? In any relationship from friendship to marriage, communication is essential for that relationship to be healthy. If there is no communication, then there is no relationship. The other six components are *Fellowship, Worship, Revelation, Meditation, Communion,* and *Intimacy.* These are all important elements to being in relationship with God. You have to have revelation because this exposes you to who He is. Once you have revelation, you get to really know Him and not just know about Him. It's a very different thing to know someone as opposed to just knowing about them. A lot of people know about God. Yet He says to them, "I never knew you."

It's only in intimacy with Him that you get revelation of who He is. It's the same way a man and woman become intimate and get to know each other. You fall in love with God through intimacy and relationship. If you want to be transformed, get in relationship with God, don't be just an associate—be in relationship!

Right Information: Hebrew 4:16; Matthew 7:23; Matthew 6:33; Psalm 97:5

Meditation:

Revelation:

Examination:

Declaration:

DAY 16

CHANGE ATTRACTS OPPOSITION

"You Shall Receive Power!"

"Be sober, be vigilant, because your adversary the devil walketh about as roaring lion, seeking whom he may devour." (1 Peter 5:8) You have to know that when you make up your mind to be transformed in the image and likeness of Christ Jesus, the enemy will try to oppose the process of your transformation. When change starts to take place, there will be opposition. After Jesus came out of the wilderness, the enemy was there, trying to oppose Him from going forth to begin to cause change to hit the nation. One thing you must know is that you have the power to move beyond the opposition. The Word declares, "But ye shall receive power, after that the Holy Ghost is come upon you" (Acts 1:8). Do you have the Holy Spirit? Well, if you do then know that you have power! Also know that "…in all these things we are more than conquerors through Him that loved us." (Romans 8:37)

You have to understand that the ones close to you will be the very ones that the enemy will try to use to oppose you and prevent you from being transformed. David had his brother Eliab and the man he looked up to, Saul, trying to oppose him from moving into the direction that God was taking him. When you have this kind of opposition coming your way, you have to know that the fight is not natural but spiritual. You will have to press past the opposition to embrace change. Some people hate change, which is why they stay in a place of comfort and conformity. Don't let other people or things keep you from transforming. Recognize the opposition and move beyond it. Jesus couldn't allow opposition to keep Him from going to the cross to save us. If people or circumstances aren't supporting your change, move them out of the way and keep moving. Not everyone will agree with your transformation but keep moving anyhow. The Bible says, "We are more than conquerors." So, a bit of opposition shall not affect you in any way. Don't let the opposition get the better of you; but rather, make sure that you get the better of the opposition! Opposition brings out more change. David said, "It was good that I was afflicted." (Psalm 119:71) Opposition can make us stronger and wiser if we allow it to. 1 Peter 5:10 states, "But the God of all grace, who hath called us unto his eternal glory by Christ Jesus, after that ye have suffered a while, make you perfect, stablish, strengthen, settle you." Use opposition for your good! Let the GREATER one on the inside of you REIGN in the midst of opposition.

The Word declares, "Ye are of God, little children, and have overcome them: because greater is He that is in you, than he that is in the world." (1 John 4:4)

Right Information: 1 Peter 5:8; Acts 1:8; Romans 8:37; 1 John 4:4

Meditation:

Revelation:

Examination:

Declaration:

DAY 17

BROKEN FOCUS

"Don't Look Back!"

Knowing that opposition will come, be careful not to lose focus on your process of transformation. When you step out into the unknown in your process of change, you will have scary moments and trying moments. You are being transformed from the inside out, and a lot of stuff will be new to you. It may seem hard or unattainable at times, but you have to know that you can do it.

You will have people and things trying to distract you from being transformed. The distractor is a giant we will continuously notice when he's lurking—and we should dismiss him when he comes. When Jesus called Peter out of the boat and onto the water, Peter asked Jesus if it was Him who was calling him out. Peter wanted something new—he wanted change. Jesus told Peter to come and; by faith, Peter stepped out of the boat and began to walk on water. I'm sure the people on the boat were telling him not to go. They were probably yelling and calling him crazy, but it did not stop Peter. He had been told to come and walk on the water by Jesus. In the midst of walking on water, he got distracted by the storm and winds that were raging around him. He took his focus off Jesus and put it on the opposition or distraction for a moment. He took his eyes off the very One who was causing change to impact his life. He lost focus!

When you're doing something new, you will have everyone and everything trying to keep you from focusing—but you have to stay focused. Stay focused on your prayer schedule, your fasting, your Bible reading, etc. Your focus is everything in the next thirteen days of change. You have to keep your eyes on the goal, which is for you to break your bad habits and be transformed into the man or woman of God that He has designed you to be. Colossians 3:2 states, "Set your affection on things above, not on things on the earth." *Affection* in Greek is *splagchnon* and it refers to a person's inward parts, the heart, the affection, the seat of feelings. You have to set your affection on Him and stay focused. Put your heart and affection into this transformation, so you don't lose your focus. If Lot's wife had stayed focused on what she had been running towards instead of being distracted, she wouldn't have turned into a pillar of salt. (See Genesis 19:26) FOCUS! Your ability to focus determines the amount of change that will be manifested in your life.

Right Information: Matthew 14:28; Colossians 3:2; Genesis 19:26

Meditation:

Revelation:

Examination:

Declaration:

DAY 18

OVERCOMING MOMENTARY FAILURE

"Let It Refine You, Not Define You"

As I stated in the beginning, change is a process. When one is transformed from the inside out, a process takes place. Remember, we talked about the butterfly. You're in one of the stages of metamorphosis, so you still have further to go. When change happens in your life, you will have mishaps or failures along the way. You may miss the mark, but you must remember that we all fall short every day. We are not perfect in our own strength, and that's why we need to boast in our weaknesses like Paul did because Jesus perfects that weakness with His strength. It's okay to mess up—but you only truly fail when you stop trying. You can't get discouraged in your process when things get frustrating, but you must overcome that moment of failure by pressing through.

Opposition will come, but try not to get discouraged by the setbacks or delays. Let them be the fire that ignites you as you endure the process. A successful person is not one who does everything right, who doesn't fail at times, who doesn't have opposition, but one who never gives up. Peter had to get his focus back. He couldn't dwell on the fact that he had become distracted and started to sink. If he had remained in that place of momentary failure, he would have missed his moment.

If David had been consumed by and had dwelt on his failures, he wouldn't have been a man after God's own heart. When he failed in integrity and holiness, he didn't dwell there, but he asked God to forgive him, and to create in him a clean heart and renew the right spirit within him. (See Psalm 51:10)

So, you can't dwell on your mistakes! You have to use them as stepping stones. YOU ARE AN OVERCOMER! Don't become your mistake, but let it make you better.

Right Information: Psalm 51

Meditation:

Revelation:

Examination:

Declaration:

DAY 19

GUARD YOUR GATES

"No Trespassing!"

When you are pursuing anything besides the norm, you have to guard your possession. Transformation is something that must be guarded. You have different gates where there can be hindrances that can cause you to go backwards in your transformation. The ear gates, eye gates, and mouth gate all have a pivotal point back to your soul. Your soul consists of your mind, will, and emotions, and it is the very thing that is being transformed in your life. You have to be careful of what you listen to, what you see, and what you say. Particularly, during these thirty days of transformation, you need to guard all three gates. You can't sit in the midst of gossip, murmuring, complaining, worldly music, etc. because all of that will negatively affect your transformation. You can't watch just anything. You have to understand that a war is happening between your spirit and your flesh. (See Galatians 5:17) Your flesh is weak, BUT your spirit is willing. You have to be willing to guard your gates so that true transformation can take place.

The imagination is powerful and creative, so if you're watching something that's not conducive to your change and puts ungodly images in your mind, then your transformation will be hindered. You have to watch your mouth. You can't be loose-lipped during these thirty days. You have to put your mouth on the altar. You have to be "...swift to hear, slow to speak, slow to wrath" (James 1:19) because "death and life are in the power of the tongue." (Proverbs 18:21)

You have the power to facilitate your transformation by speaking words of life. With the same mouth, you can hinder or destroy your change. You have to get into a habit of speaking life into the situation. We are so used to saying whatever we want to say, but when you want change to impact your life, you have to be careful not to speak against it.

You also have to guard your mind by being careful about what you think and meditate on. You need to form a habit of thinking on "whatsoever things are true, whatsoever things are honest, whatsoever things are just, whatsoever things are pure, whatsoever things are lovely, whatsoever things are of good report; if there be any virtue, and if there be any praise, think on these things." (Philippians 4:8) If your thoughts do not align with these guidelines then you need to start casting down some thoughts. "As a man thinketh in his heart so is he." (Proverbs 23:7) If you think defeated, you will be defeated. "He has given us the power to cast down every vain imagination that exalts itself against the knowledge of God." (2 Corinthians 10:5) Guard your gates because it's necessary for your transformation.

Right Information: James 1:19; Proverbs 18:21; Philippians 4:8; Proverbs 23:7; 2 Corinthians 10:5

Meditation:

Revelation:

Examination:

Declaration:

DAY 20

DEAL WITH YOUR ROOTS

"Stop Medicating Your Symptoms!"

This is where the real work begins. If you truly want to be transformed from the inside out, you are going to have to deal with your inner self. Inner healing and deliverance are subjects that are overlooked in the church, but they are so necessary for us to be transformed in His image and likeness. A lot of times, we stay the way we are and never change because we never deal with the real cause of our issues which is the root. We tend to deal with the different symptoms or branches of the tree to feel better, but often find ourselves right back, dealing with the issue because the root was never dealt with. The true power of a thing is in its root or foundation. A tree's roots give it strength to stand upright. The branches can get cut off, but they will grow right back in a season because the root is still there.

We try to medicate different issues in our life by getting counseling, therapists, psychologists, doctors, etc. but I have bad news for you: your issue is still there. The problem is not the things you can see but the unseen things…the root.

Don't be afraid to invest in your transformation by opening up your *alabaster box* to reveal what's behind the image you display to the world. The woman with the alabaster box brought all she had to Jesus. The oil inside her box was a very expensive oil. Her offering cost her a lot. (See Luke 7:37-38) We all have things within that have cost us dearly. Things such as tears, pain, suffering, bitterness, unforgiveness, hate, anger, and maybe much more. We have to get to the place where we are desperate enough to get out of the bondage and negative cycles, and bring all of it to God. Open up to God. He knows your past, present and future, so you can be open with Him. We try to cover the bruises and scars with masks, smiles, clothes, shoes, cars, jobs, etc. but after all the pretending, when you get by yourself, your wounds and pain will still speak to you.

If you want to be a true servant and disciple of God, you have to get your old roots uprooted and cut away. He can't build and plant within if your roots are still intact. Go back to the roots and let God cut them away. The woman with the alabaster box was labeled as a sinner, but God called her forgiven. Because she had decided to deal with her roots, the inner issues that were expressed through her outer expression, she was made whole and forgiven. Glory be to God! There is no greater thing than real freedom which comes after the roots have been dealt with.

We have to go to God and say, "Here I am, I bring my alabaster box, and I give it to You. I choose to be free." A lot of times, we would rather hide in the midst of our pain, hurt, bitterness, or anger just to keep love from entering into that place. Let me tell you, there is not one person, place, or thing that is worth sacrificing your transformed life for. That's why I started with the section on knowing your worth. You have to know that you're valuable, and that there is treasure within you that God wants to show to the world. I encourage you to go deeper and let God deal with YOU. Take the mask off and come forward with everything to God. If the root of the problem is not uprooted, you can't come into your full transformation. So, let's deal with the roots!

Why are you so angry?
Why do you reject love?
Why do you keep to yourself?
Why don't you trust anyone?

Is it because you were abandoned as a child, or is it because the last relationship you were in caused you so much pain that you chose not to love again? Is it because you were molested as a child, so you don't trust people? Why are you the way you are? Why do you do what you do? You have to ask yourself honestly and honestly respond. There is a root reason why you are the way you are…let's deal with it!

Right Information: Luke 7:37; Mark 14:3; Matthew 26:7

Meditation:

Revelation:

Examination:

Declaration:

DAY 21

MATTERS OF THE HEART

"Issues of Life"

Our English word *heart* comes from the Greek word *kardia*, which means, "the seat of self." That is, the true self. "The heart is deceitful above all things, and desperately wicked." (Jeremiah 17:9) In the beginning, God created man, gave him a commandment that he failed to obey, and he lost his power, possession, and land. He lost it all. Because of one man's disobedience, we all became sinners. We are all born and shaped in iniquity which is why we have to be born again. Because we are born sinners, our hearts are wicked and evil…who can know it? We don't know the capacity of evil that resides in our heart before we are born again. When we are born again, we have to ask for a new heart. It states in Ezekiel 36:26, "A new heart also will I give you, and a new spirit will I put within you: and I will take away the stony heart out of your flesh, and I will give you a heart of flesh."

Have you asked for a new heart? Coming into the Kingdom of God, we have banged up hearts that need our Savior. The true self resides there. A lot of times, we forfeit transformation because our heart is wicked. God states that many hearts will grow cold in the last days. (See Matthew 24:12) That's why for true transformation to come forth in your life, you have to encounter God and be baptized in the love of God to transform your heart. "Keep thy heart with all diligence; for out of it are the issues of life." (Proverbs 4:23) Your mouth speaks from the heart, so you know what's in your heart by how you speak. A lot of issues that reside in the heart stem from a lack of true agape love. We often look to people to impart the love in vacant places, hurting places, etc., and when they don't follow through, we begin to build issues on that. A transformed heart is one that has been baptized in the love of God. Your lack of change could be from an issue of the heart. What's in your heart affects every aspect of your life.

You have to go broken and contrite before God with a willingness to let go and be free, asking Him to create in you a clean heart. You have to be willing to forgive. We carry so much in our hearts that it affects us, not only spiritually but naturally as well. When our heart is filled with hate, strife, anger, bitterness, and unforgiveness, it affects our body, soul, spirit, and our whole life. We have to allow God to detox our heart. Ask God to go into your heart and bring healing, deliverance, and restoration. Be willing, obedient, and ready to do what He asks of you.

Right Information: Jeremiah 17:9; Ezekiel 36:26; Matthew 24:12; Proverbs 4:23

Meditation:

Revelation:

Examination:

Declaration:

DAY 22

DIE TO SELF

"It's Not About You!"

I have heard it said, "to get something you've never had, you have to do something you've never done." This is usually a touchy topic because we have a lot of people who are stuck in the way they do things in the Kingdom of God. When you enter the Kingdom of God, you no longer live this new life in Christ Jesus the way you want to. You now have stepped into the purpose which God created you for a specified assignment. You now have to depend on Him. We are very independent before we come into Christ. We are used to doing things our way, thinking our way, walking our way, talking our way…but now, it's time to let someone else take the wheel. His name is Jesus!

Paul stated, "It's no longer 'I' that lives, but CHRIST who lives in me." He could state that boldly because he was no longer doing what Paul wanted to do, but he did the will of the One he was submitted and surrendered to. If you want change, you must change first. You must die to yourself to be transformed. Jesus said, "If any man will come after me, let him deny himself, and take up his cross daily, and follow me."

(Luke 9:23) A lot of times, we try picking up the cross, but we don't deny our flesh. The cross, metaphorically speaking, represents the work of the kingdom. We see people trying to do kingdom business, but there is no display of Jesus Christ. Why? Because there is no death to self. If you truly want change and want to live a transformed life, you have to truly DIE TO YOURSELF! You have to yield all your rights to the Holy Spirit. You have to walk by the Spirit and not after this flesh. This is how you will not fulfill the lust of the flesh. Choose to submit your will to His will. True death to self is the yielding of your will and the submission to God's will. Sometimes, we forfeit it because we'd rather be prideful and live. We'd rather not be wrong and live. We'd rather say what we want and live. We'd rather do what we want and how we want and live! The list goes on. We have to make up in our mind, "I will die for Christ, so He can live in me."

You can't live a transformed life and at the same time do what you want, what you feel, and what you think. You will never come into the fullness of transformation with your flesh on display. Paul said, "I beat my flesh daily, so that I won't be a cast away. He also declared, "I bring my body under subjection." (1 Corinthians 9:27) Why? He had to die to himself so that Christ could live in him. He then could say, "I am crucified with Christ: nevertheless, I live; yet not I, but Christ liveth in me…" (Galatians 2:20) He chose to yield all his rights to the Holy Spirit. He chose to give up his will for God's will.

Jesus did the same. He had a desire to please God with His life. At a place of pain, suffering, and agony, Jesus chose to give His will over for God's will. He said, "God, if it be Your will, let this cup pass." Because this was what He desired—for the cup of suffering to pass Him by. He then said, "nevertheless not my will but Your will be done." You have to mortify the deeds and ways of the flesh if you want change to come. You can't always be right, and you have to be okay with being wrong. Deny your flesh AND THEN pick up your cross and follow the example of Jesus Christ and be transformed. Confess it "I CHOOSE TO DIE!"

Right Information: Luke 9:23; 1 Corinthians 9:27; Galatians 2:20

Meditation:

Revelation:

Examination:

Declaration:

DAY 23

GET SUPPORT

"I Need You!"

Make sure you get support. Surround yourself with like-minded people who are living a transformed life or who are pursuing a transformed life. Get an accountability partner. You want to have support because it will seem unbearable at times when you start something new. I know when I decided to transform my life into a healthy one, I had to have a support system to keep me encouraged. You want to have someone to run with you just in case you feel like giving up. It's important for you to endure the next seven days without giving up. I want to encourage you. You have made it this far…so, congratulations! I am proud of you. I hope your life has been impacted since starting this book. I want you to know that "you can do all things through Christ which strengthens you." (See Philippians 4:13) You've got this! Let's finish this! You can use this day to recap any of the previous days you want to refresh yourself on. You can use this day to recap and meditate on Scriptures. However you decide to use this day, make the most of it.

Kendra Watkins

Right Information: Philippians 4:13

Meditation:

Revelation:

Examination:

Declaration:

DAY 24

FEAR DOWN, FAITH UP!

"No Fear! He Will Lead You"

When it comes to change, it can be a scary process because you are outside of your norm. If change is to have any chance of impacting your life, you must move in faith. When you change your mindset and environment, you're on an unknown journey. The things that were once your go-to comforts are now behind you because you have chosen to change. Now that you have had the courage and boldness to allow change to transform your life, you're now in the unknown which is the best place to be. You're now in a place where God can lead you, and He desires to lead you straight into destiny. He has purpose for your life.

Now, I want to encourage you to "walk by faith and not by sight." (See 2 Corinthians 5:7) When you're in an unknown place, it's possible to miss steps because it's new. I want you to keep the faith and keep moving in obedience. The Israelites trusted God to be their guide. They were led by a cloud in the day and a pillar of fire by night. They moved in faith as they trusted Moses' ability to hear God. They walked out of bondage in Egypt because they decided to follow the voice of God through Moses. They didn't fear! Even when they came to a place where it seemed like there wasn't anywhere else to go, they stood still in faith to see the hand of God move on their behalf. Moses declared, "Fear ye not, stand still, and see the salvation of the Lord, which he will shew to you to day." (Exodus 14:13)

We must have that same mindset and attitude in life when it comes to change. We must trust the direction God has given us, and we have to move even though we may not understand where we are going.

One thing I know is, "For my thoughts are not your thoughts, neither are your ways my ways…" (Isaiah 55:8) so we can't allow our limited thinking to keep the unlimited mindset of God from moving in our lives. It takes faith for change to manifest in your life, now that you've decided to move into a place that wasn't known to you before. Hebrews 11:1 declares, "Now faith is the substance of things hoped for, the evidence of things not seen." If faith has a substance and evidence, then that means that whatever we are hoping for will materialize. You just have to trust God. You can't allow fear of the unknown to keep you from change. Fear is bondage all by itself as well as a spirit. Fear keeps you from your purpose and destiny. 2 Timothy 1:7 states, "For God hath not given us the spirit of fear; but of power, and of love, and of a sound mind." That's why we talked about how your mindset has to change. You have to be endowed with power from on high, and the love of God that casts out fear has to be encountered. Don't opt out of what God is doing because fear tries to keep you out. Trust God and keep going just like the Israelites did. Don't let fear keep you from going further. Don't limit yourself to how far you can go!

Right Information: 2 Corinthians 5:7; Exodus 14:13; Isaiah 55:8; Hebrews 11:1; 2 Timothy 1:7

Meditation:

Revelation:

Examination:

Declaration:

DAY 25

ENDURE THE PROCESS

"Persevere!"

You've made it this far. Keep pressing on! I want you to know how far you have come and I want you to continue to press on in spite of physical or spiritual opposition. Many times, we are so close to our breakthrough, but then trials and tribulations come and beset us. The Scripture says, "And let us not be weary in well doing: for in due season we shall reap, if we faint not." (Galatians 6:9) You can't faint.

The woman with the issue of blood had been bleeding for twelve years before she was able to get her healing. (See Luke 8) She had heard that Jesus was in town, and she proceeded to get to Him. I can only imagine how discouraged she was, but there was something within her that caused her to continue to look for the healing she desired. She could have given up a long time ago when the doctors had said that there was no cure, but she endured the process to her healing that happened immediately when she encountered Jesus. Now, in those days, it was illegal for a woman like her to be in the gates, but she was so desperate that she did not allow that to keep her from getting what she had been longing for. She pressed past the crowd, which can represent opposition. She pressed through people who told her she would never be healed, people who gave up on her, family who disowned her, hindrances, and barriers that had been designed to cause her to give up in her process to her healing. She didn't allow negativity to keep her from possessing what she desired. She had this in her heart: "If I could just touch the hem of His garment, I know that I will be made whole." (See Matthew 9:21) Just visualize the crowd that she was in the midst of. She had people pushing her and trying to move ahead of her to get to Jesus. She persevered in her press to touch the hem of His garment. She knew that if she touched it, it would make her whole. She finally touched it! Immediately, she was made whole!

But it didn't stop there…Jesus asked who had touched Him. The disciples thought it was crazy that He was asking such a thing in the midst of a crowd of people who were all trying to get to Him. He knew that virtue had left Him. She got the attention of Jesus. She persevered and she stumbled over into the breakthrough that she had been seeking for twelve long years. This is the power of perseverance. I encourage you today to persevere. Don't stop now! Continue the process of your journey of transformation. You are setting yourself up for something that will change your life for the better. I am reminded of the widow who kept on coming to the unjust judge. She finally got what she desired by her perseverance. (See Luke 18)

Keep getting up daily and spending time with God and using this devotional, and you will get the very thing your heart desires. Don't lose heart! Don't give up! Persevere!

Right Information: Luke 8; Matthew 9:21; Luke 18

Meditation:

Revelation:

Examination:

Declaration:

DAY 26

WHO ELSE IS IN THE FIRE?

"Untouched!"

The story of the three Hebrew boys always brings great insight about how to trust God with your life. When change begins in your life, you know that opposition will come as we discussed earlier in these thirty days. For change to be sustained in your life, there is a purging that God must do to perfect things in your life. The fiery trials and tribulations are always in your life for a PURPOSE. There is a reason for what you are going through right now. You have to understand that God does nothing without purpose. There is PURPOSE in everything our Father does. The Word declares, "To everything there is a season, and a time to **every purpose** under the heaven." (Ecclesiastes 3:1)

When God allows anything to happen in your life, He knows that you're able to overcome it! How? Because He put the overcomer within you. The trial was never meant to get the best of you, but you were meant to get the best of it. The fiery trials that Peter talks about are to consume what is necessary for God to transform you into the image and likeness of Jesus Christ. This is His original intention.

When Satan came to God about Job, God gave him the right to go and try Job. It wasn't that God didn't love Job or wanted him to suffer, but he wanted Job to see what he had on the inside of him. However, one thing that is necessary is to make sure you keep your focus and mind on the One who helps you through it. The three Hebrew boys stayed focused on who God was the whole time, which caused the fire not to harm them but to benefit them.

We discussed this story earlier in Day 12. After holding on to what they believed, they were thrown into a fiery furnace which was naturally designed to destroy them, but spiritually, God was doing something greater. They kept their eyes on the One who was able to deliver them. Because they kept their focus on the Deliverer in the midst of the fiery trial, they were accompanied by God Himself and walked out of the fire untouched. That trial got them promotion. On the other hand, Job had to get his focus together. He had his moments of throwing a fit, but he took his focus off the natural and began to do according to the Kingdom of God. It wasn't until he began to pray for his friends that Job's life shifted for the better. You have to make sure the purpose of the fire is evident in your life. Remember your trials and tribulations has a purpose.

Right Information: Daniel 3:1-30; Ecclesiastes 3:1

Meditation:

Revelation:

Examination:

Declaration:

DAY 27

MAKE A DEPOSIT

"Inwardly Perishing"

When change is happening in your life, you must understand that you are coming out of the norm of things. Change takes you into the new. When you encounter something new, you have to learn how to embrace this new thing that you have. It's just like going to a new city or a place you have never been before. You grew up in a totally different city for most of your life; now you have to gain knowledge and information about this new city in which you now reside. You learn about the people, places, and things in this new place. As you are being transformed into the intended idea that God has for you, you have to learn who you are now. You have to find out who you really are on the inside. Introduce you to yourself.

The way this takes place is that you make a deposit in yourself. Deposit the Word of God. You have to deposit time with God. Deposit time in the presence of the saints, as well as sacrificing the biggest thing we have, and that's our time. Time alone with God to impart the very nature, attributes, and ways of God in yourself. We spend so much time investing outwardly and trying to play a part in life. We spend time trying to remodel or remake the very thing that God wants to remold into the original intent He had at the beginning. Because we spend so much time on the outward appearance, we lack so much inwardly. Inwardly, we are jacked up. Understand that true change begins on the inside. We try to make it happen outwardly by effort, when the very change that is taking place outwardly will not last because nothing ever happened inwardly to be the source of that change. Your heart has to change before your works do! Your works will change when your heart changes.

The most important deposit is the Word of God. You have heard Romans 12:1 and 2 repeated over and over throughout this process. Why? Because it is essential for the change and transformation. It's the Word that has the power to divide the soul from the spirit. It's the Word that washes and cleanses us. It's the Word that has the ability to break the chains of lies. Jeremiah said that God's Word is like fire and a hammer. A hammer can do some damage if you use it. The Word is going to break the web of lies. If you forsake the depositing of the Word in yourself, you will find yourself back at the beginning and worse off than before.

Right Information: Matthew 12:24-26; Joshua 1:8; Psalms 1:1-3

Meditation:

Revelation:

Examination:

Declaration:

DAY 28

TEMPORARY CHANGE

A Will Surrendered

When you don't let go COMPLETELY, your change will be limited and temporary. In order for change or transformation to have its full effect, one must be totally surrendered in obedience. You have to understand that not letting go completely is the same as not letting go at all. Not letting go completely is related to the spirit of disobedience.

As an example, let's look at the story of Saul. Saul was given specific instructions to go and kill all the Amalekites. He decided to not fully do what had been asked of him. He was more concerned about what the people thought than about being obedient to the Spirit of the Lord. He could only go so far because he didn't completely let go of himself. When I speak of "letting go of himself," I mean that he was not willing to die to his own will and do what he had been told. What was to take place was limited and temporary because he didn't totally obey. I've heard it said, "A little leaven leavens the whole lump." That is why his actions cost him dearly. He went no further than where he was that moment in his life. He lost everything because he decided not to let go completely.

In comparison to someone having the choice to put his will in the way, let's look at a great example. Jesus was put in the same position as Saul. He was also given a specific assignment. He had a moment in His life to allow His will to intersect with the plan of God. Jesus had to know that if He didn't fully let go of Himself, that transformation wouldn't be able to take place for the next generation. In the most trying moment of His life, He chose to let go of His own will completely and let God's will be done. In the Garden of Gethsemane, Jesus cried out, "Lord, let this cup pass from me if it can, but nevertheless NOT MY WILL BE DONE BUT YOUR WILL BE DONE." He chose to let go completely, so that the will of the Father could be done.

It's when they let go completely that you see the manifested hand of God in a person's life. Because Jesus chose to let go of Himself, we have the benefit today of the exchange at the cross. Now, I'm not only speaking of letting go of self when I speak of letting go for change or transformation to take place in your life. There can be different things you hold on to that can hinder, limit, or cause only temporary change to take place in your life. You can have relationships that you know God has specifically told you to walk away from. You have said your goodbyes, but you still call or text here and there. Perhaps you still chat on social media. That's not totally letting go. When you are still in connection, you are still in relationship with that individual. It doesn't even have to be a relationship. It could be a job, a place, or a thing, but whatever it is, you have to decide to totally LET GO! When you hold back, you hold back your own change or transformation.

Let's look at the story of Lot and his wife. Lot and his wife were told to leave the place they were living and to let go totally. They were even told NOT TO LOOK BACK! Looking back does not do anything but keep you from moving forward and possessing what's ahead of you. Lot and his wife were out of the city already, but she decided to look back. That moment of looking back caused her change that was taking place to be temporary. She turned into a pillar of salt. She went no further from that place.

Decide today that as change or transformation is taking place in your life, that you will let go of whatever is necessary to keep and continue that transformation. Remember you have worth—so, if it is necessary for you to let go of anything, then you can be sure that there is something better coming. "I have a past, but the past doesn't have me," are words spoken by TD Jakes. That's what our mentality has to be. Our past can no longer have us.

Right Information: 1 Samuel 15; Genesis 19:17-26

Meditation:

Revelation:

Examination:

Declaration:

DAY 29

NO FORMS

"Be the Change!"

Don't fake it till you make it. Go ahead and BE THE CHANGE! Your pretending will get you the lead performance. You will become the character you once acted. Do not spend your life trying to become something by pretending. *Pretending* or acting is done from the outside. *Becoming* is done from the inside.

The Word says that we are not to put on a form of godliness. The one who puts on just the form is the one who's pretending or acting by what they see. *Pretend* means, "to speak and act so as to make it appear that something is the case when in fact it is not or not really what it is represented as being; used in a game or deception." Putting on the forms of something falls into the same category as deception.

True transformation cannot be faked. If it's not from the heart, it will not last or be legit. You don't want to fake it. You want God to transform and change you for real. It's important to examine yourself. It's important to let the Word of God that's like a sword pierce you. The forms or pretending can only be avoided by being who you truly are. Be who God has called you to be. Don't be like the Sadducees and Pharisees who didn't come out of religion or tradition, so they put on the forms. According to Matthew 3:8, when John saw the Pharisees and Sadducees coming to his baptism, he called them a generation of vipers. Vipers are snakes which represent deception. Pretending was defined as a form of deception. He said to them, "bring forth (show me) therefore fruits meet for repentance." Why? Because there was no transformation with them.

As you read earlier in the book, we know that true repentance brings a change of mind and direction. Their minds had not changed and neither had their actions. They were still operating according to the old ways. Putting on forms means doing stuff out of religion and obligation, which is what they were doing. When you pretend, it is evidence of not having a true revelation of your salvation or of who you really are in Jesus Christ. Don't put on a show like you have it all together. It's okay to get help and even to be wrong. You have to be okay with not knowing how, so you can be shown the right way by the Holy Spirit. We rather pretend like we're cool and this gets us in forms. I declare transformation is your portion as you renew your mind. Remember: no forms; be transformed!

Right Information: 2 Timothy 3:5-7; Romans 12:1-2

Meditation:

Revelation:

Examination:

Declaration:

DAY 30

WHAT DO YOU SEE?

"God's Perspective vs. Your Perspective"

As all this change take place, you have to see yourself as you are changed now. If you hold onto a poor image of yourself, you will never strive above or beyond what you see. If you can see it, you will at some point go in that direction. Change will not have an impact on your environment if you don't create it properly, so how you think creates the environment. Your perspective is everything to your transformation. Your perspective or what you see is in connection with the heart and mind. Your heart has eyes. When you see within your heart, it is an image that works within the mind, and that works with your words and actions. We need to open our eyes to change. We must ask God to open our eyes to see.

Elisha prayed to God, "Open his eyes, Lord, so that he may see." It wasn't that he was blind naturally. He wanted him to see what he saw within His heart. At this moment, Elisha wanted his servant to see that they were protected and had backup. They were being attacked by a king who was mad. They surrounded their city with chariots and horses. The servant of Elisha basically asked him, "What do we have?" Elisha told him, "Fear not: for they that be with us are more than they that be with them." Elisha must have discerned his servant's doubt and worry because he prayed to God afterwards. What he saw was bigger than what surrounded him. What he saw did not come naturally, but spiritually from the heart. How you see and what you see is important if change is to take place. If Elisha had seen only the ambush that had been set up against him, he would have been defeated. He saw what he desired with his heart. Because he saw with his heart, he spoke and assured his servant that they were well protected. Though Elisha didn't see this naturally, he was confident that they were protected. He saw with his heart which worked his imagination to see the great army they had. He then spoke and created reality with his mouth in faith by letting his servant know that he didn't have to fear. He then acted on what he had seen and believed. He didn't back away in fear but stepped forward in expectation of what he was seeing. Elisha prayed to the Lord that the army would be smitten with blindness. The Scripture states, "And He smote them with blindness according to the word of Elisha." Do you see how what he saw caused him to speak and act in faith? According to his word, the manifestation of what he had seen in the spirit was caused to manifest in the natural.

    You have to see the change you desire. You have to speak in alignment with what you see. You can't say that you see change, but your words state a different thing. See what you desire! Imagine it! Then you must speak and act accordingly to what you see. Begin to see the change before it happens in the natural. Speak like the change. Be the change! Ask God to "open my eyes to behold wondrous things in your Word."

Kendra Watkins

Right Information: 2 Kings 6:17; Jeremiah 1:11, 24:3; Zechariah 5:2; Amos 8:2; Psalm 119:17-24

Meditation:

Revelation:

Examination:

Declaration:

DAY 31

SURPRISE! A BONUS DAY JUST FOR YOU!

BELIEVE IN YOURSELF!
"Faith It from Here"

Wow! Look how far you have come. You have made it to this last day! I am very proud of you! Now, it's important to apply this last chapter from this day forward. Now that you are getting ready to end this thirty-day journey, your belief from this day onwards is important! You have to believe in yourself from this day forward. Belief happens in the heart. The words you say are the result of what you believe in your heart. TD Jakes said it like this: "He can use your incompetence, just not your unbelief." To believe is to accept something as true, even without proof. Only if one believes in something can one act purposefully.

Abraham believed and was fully persuaded of what God had told him and shown him. Romans 4:21 states, "And being fully persuaded that, what he had promised, he was able also to perform."

Right Information: Genesis 15:6; Galatians 3:6; Romans 4:3

    These Scriptures show us that Abraham's belief in God and in His Word was credited to him as righteousness. When you believe in God first and you can also believe in yourself, then that's a place from which you can be transformed. Stay in that place. How do you believe? Who do you believe? How do you see? What do you see? All of this is going to play a part in your life from here onwards. You have to keep on believing and trusting in God. You have to see with the eyes of faith. Remember that change is a process, and that you will need to continue to walk it out in faith. You have to see exactly what you desire and not just your current state or condition. See beyond that! When you believe, you don't yet have the full proof of its reality. That's okay! You believe even though you may not see it in the natural. Still believe! Abraham believed in what God had said, and he believed in himself. That's why he could get up from the place he was and begin to walk in the direction God was telling him would be his. When he came to the land of Canaan, it was occupied by people. He still believed God from that situation. Although in the natural, he saw that the place that had been promised to him was occupied, he did not shift his focus off what God had said. He still believed.

    Change or transformation has begun in your life! Believe it! Believe in what God has given to you and done in you the last thirty days. This is just the start of your new journey. Stay on this journey no matter how things or people may seem. God has great things in store for you. He called Abraham and what he had promised manifested. Know that you are an overcomer, and that change is your portion. Believe in yourself no matter who doesn't agree. God fearfully and wonderfully made you, and He has the expectation for you to BE GREAT in Him! Take what God has given you—and live! Be the change you want to see! Be the change the world needs! Yes, it will start with you!

Declare: I AM CHANGE!

Meditate and recap each day.

Be the change you want to see!

ACKNOWLEDGMENTS

I first give the utmost honor, praise, and thanks to My Daddy, "Abba" Father. I know this journey would not be possible without Him. I give a special thanks to my Periscope family, who encouraged this first book out of many. I thank my mentors and apostles, Cynthia and Frankie Jefferson, who made me aware of my ability to be an author and who told me that I could! I thank my best friend, Psalmist Shay Adams, who was my right-hand woman—pushing me through the process, sending emails, setting deadlines, editing, and so much more. I thank my brother in Christ, Minister Vincent Casey, who encouraged, spoke life, and helped edit this book. My sister, Teacher Chanell, who kept refreshing the God-breathed words in my life so that I could write and finish them! I also thank my brother, Dwayne Watkins Jr., who has no idea of the impact of the words he whispered to me in the last month of 2016: "GO AND BE GREAT!" Lastly, to my parents Dwayne and Jessie Watkins, who raised me in the way that I should go, I say, "THANK YOU!"

AUTHOR'S BIO

Kendra Watkins is one of the dynamic, prophetic voices God has raised up for the end times. She walks in the supernatural power of God to heal the sick, cast out devils, and perform miracles. She was born and raised in Muskegon, Michigan and later, in the year 2006, she relocated to Georgia. After this relocation, she joined Eagles Fire International Ministries, whose covering apostle is Guillermo Maldonado. In this ministry, God began to transform, train, and equip Kendra for the nations. In 2010, she was ordained as a minister. Four years later, she was ordained as a prophetess; and shortly after that, she was charged to go out to the nations. She mentors and has taught numerous classes on the apostolic anointing, the prophetic, intercessory prayer, and more. Her passion is to please God and to see His people set free and pushed into their purpose and destiny. She has been called to set the captives free through her Spirit-led preaching, teaching, and demonstration of the supernatural that brings Heaven here and now!

CONTACT THE AUTHOR

Email: Prophetesskendraministries@gmail.com

Phone: 762-233-9373

Website: Prophetesskendraministries.org

www.ingramcontent.com/pod-product-compliance
Lightning Source LLC
Chambersburg PA
CBHW072059290426
44110CB00014B/1747